T0113817

As I Remember

Lynn McKinney

**"Alzheimer's disease robs the memory
but not the memories"**

authorHOUSE®

AuthorHouse™
1663 Liberty Drive
Bloomington, IN 47403
www.authorhouse.com
Phone: 1 (800) 839-8640

Published by AuthorHouse 10/14/2015

ISBN: 978-1-5049-5247-7 (sc)
ISBN: 978-1-5049-5246-0 (e)

Print information available on the last page.

Contents

Acknowledgment

This book is dedicated to all of my siblings but especially to Lois. Your dedicated and loving care towards Mama started long before Alzheimer's.

Foreword

I had heard of Alzheimer's but I had never really put any thought into what all the symptoms of the disease were. When I was little I would hear older people talk about someone who had lost their mind. The older people didn't know what was going on either. All they knew was that someone had forgotten where they lived or maybe forgotten who their family members were. I even remember the older people saying that someone went to the "crazy house". In the Baptist choirs we often sang songs thanking the Lord that we woke up "clothed in our right mind". It wasn't until Mama was stricken with Alzheimer's that I realized what we had been singing about for all those years.

Mental illness is a topic that wasn't taken as serious as other diseases. The mental debilitations were not as obvious as someone who had cancer or diabetes. You could feel a lump with cancer.

You can see the fainting or feel your sugar level when it goes up with diabetes. We couldn't see Mama's mental condition begin to deteriorate. We didn't know that when items kept disappearing into a black hole, Alzheimer's was giving us warning signals.

Mama struggled with an enemy that she didn't know of. She was good at fixing up home remedies to take care of just about anything but Alzheimer's is one that she could not come up with a home remedy for. I believe that if Mama had known about Alzheimer's and that it was the enemy that caused people not to stay in their right mind, she would have tried to come up with a remedy. Mama was helpless.

When I look back on some of the symptoms that Mama was having, I wonder if I would have wanted to know. I know that this sounds selfish but I believe that there would have been a lot of sadness. I probably would have cried a lot just knowing how the symptoms would progress and that one day my Mama would not recognize me.

My brother and sisters and I just didn't know. The symptoms were right there in front of us. To think that we are college educated and all of us allowed Alzheimer's to overtake Mama without putting up a good fight is heartbreaking. Once we knew what was going on, we tried to fight it but Alzheimer's was too much for all of us.

I have beaten myself up many times about not knowing and for allowing a stranger to take control of Mama. I try not to entertain these thoughts for too long because if Mama were in her right mind, she would tell me not to question anything that the Lord has control over. She would tell me to just pray for her and pray for her family to be strong.

Sallie Mae McKinney is her family's earthly anchor. Her life has been blessed and through her life she has blessed her family. I have so many wonderful memories of Mama that I never want to forget. It is for this reason that I began the project of writing this book. While I can remember clearly, I want to put some of my memories in writing so that my children and others in the McKinney family will keep the memories of Sallie and Raymond McKinney going.

I am also writing this book as a tribute to all victims of Alzheimer's. There are so many wonderful men women in nursing homes who are loved and who need to be remembered. This book is a challenge or rather a plea to the children and other family members of these mothers and fathers in nursing homes, to write down some of your precious memories in an "I Remember" journal. I hope to see "I Remember" journals from all over the world sharing the memories of their love ones as I have shared with you in this book. Believe me, your journal will become a precious treasure to you as mine is to me. My journal makes me want to speak to Alzheimer's as if it were a person. I want to tell Alzheimer's that I got you back for what you stole from my Mama. I want to say to Alzheimer's "you stole Mama's memory but you didn't steal the memories". The memories are forever.

MAMA

Sweet Potato Tears

Sweet Potato Tears

To the best of my knowledge, onions were the only vegetable that brought tears to your eyes. This notion proved to be incorrect as I stood over a bowl of sweet potatoes with tears streaming down my face. Some of the tears dripped on to the potatoes.

I had gotten up that morning with a little bit of excitement about preparing and baking my first sweet potato pie. I thought for sure that I knew how to make one even though I had never baked one before. I watched Mama many times as a girl making her famous potato pies. Whenever I got old enough to handle a sharp knife, Mama would let me, or should I say, Mama would make me peel the sweet potatoes. As I got older, there was no need to "make me" because I enjoyed being in the kitchen with Mama as she cooked.

Mama never said how much of anything she was putting in her dishes. As a matter of fact, I doubt if she owned a measuring spoon or cup. Somehow she just knew how much. Watching Mama cook was like watching Michelangelo paint. She cooked with ease and so quickly and smoothly. There would be a pot or a skillet on every burner of the stove. The only timer that she would use was the one in her head. Mama knew when each pot had started and she knew when to turn the fire off of each. Mama worked it out so that everything came together around the same time.

My sisters and I have often tried to solve the mystery of the "Mama taste". Everything and I do mean everything, that Mama cooked was simply delicious. I know that there had to be some days when Mama was short of one of the ingredients but somehow she sealed her taste into each dish. She could make mustard greens taste like a rich delicacy. Her cornbread made you forget the rest of the meal. I was often content with a little buttered syrup and a piece of Mama's cornbread.

On this particular morning, I am thinking back on the days of growing up on Sandidge Road in Orange Mound, Mississippi. I am thinking that back then I didn't know how blessed I was to have such a strong Christian, fun-loving, courageous mother. Sallie Mae McKinney, my mama has always been so much wrapped up in one mind and one body. Mama seemed to always know what to say to a problem. She counseled not only her own children, but her sisters, brothers, neighbors, friends, and whomever.

Mama taught herself how to sew. I'm not talking about hemming a pair of pants. Mama became quite a good seamstress. She made the curtains for each window of the house. She loved quilting. Her older sister, Hattie, taught her quilting. They would often allow me to add a finishing touch here and there like tying up the decorative yarn or sewing on buttons. This is one of the reasons that I have grown to love craft work such as knitting, crocheting, and sewing.

Mama was a self-employed painter. It was nothing to come home and find that Mama had painted a bedroom or added borders at the top, side, bottom, or wherever she thought looked creative. I remember deciding to paint the foyer of my home. I thought about how Mama used to paint and decided that I would give it a try. Originally, I had planned to paint the foyer and two other rooms. By the time I had finished with the foyer, I had a new found respect for the painting professionals. I had an even deeper respect for Mama. She made it look so easy. I was exhausted after one room. She had to have been exhausted but we would never know it.

Mama has always been a gardener. You will find a picture of her in the archives of the local paper, *The DeSoto Times*. Her story in the newspaper was nothing short of incredible. Mama planted some sweet potatoes in a small section of soil near the main garden. Daddy went along with her idea to plant but doubted that anything would grow. That was a characteristic of my father. He always built Mama up when she did something that the average person would not try. Mama nurtured and doctored on her sweet potatoes as if they could understand her sweetness when she talked to them each day. Mama made sure that her potatoes got enough water. She kept an eye out for any of the animals that might be looking for a sweet tasty meal. Mama's potatoes not only grew, they grew to the point that you couldn't pick one up with only one hand. One of her potatoes weighed over eight pounds and this is what landed Mama in the newspaper.

We often told each other (my sisters, brother, and I) that Mama was an entrepreneur before her time. Mama has always had some kind of honest business going on, on the side. She has catered fancy dinners and baked cakes and pies that I would not dare attempt to number.

Mama was so proud and happy to own and operate "Sallie's Kitchen". Sallie's Kitchen was located right off of Highway 78. Highway 78 connected Orange Mound to Memphis in only a few minutes drive. People would drive from Memphis and all around to get one of Mama's catfish dinners or for one of the famous "McKinney Burgers". When Mama finally closed "Sallie's Kitchen", she had gotten her money's worth as well as her satisfaction out of it. Dianne, the youngest of the children, had finished college so Mama's purpose for the restaurant had run its course. There are many wonderful memories of working at "Sallie's Kitchen". My family and friends get to enjoy the famous "McKinney Burger every now and then.

Mama was always an active member of the National Association for the Advancement of Colored People (NAACP), yet she had almost as many white friends as blacks. To many, Mama was the NAACP. Whenever anyone got arrested or in trouble they would send for Mrs. Sallie Mae. Mama has gone to court with so many people. She wasn't afraid to speak to any attorney or judge. Mama knew every big shot white person in Orange Mound. All of them had eaten her famous cooking at one time or the other because Mama was the head chef at the Orange Mound Country Club. Dr. Martin Luther King, Jr would have loved Mama because she would have marched with him and then she would have taken him home and fed him some of her delicious cooking.

Mama and Daddy welcomed everyone to our home. I still wonder where everyone slept. My friends loved to spend the night over to the McKinney's. There was always good food and plenty of hearty laughs. Mama was a true comedian in our growing up years and all through the years before Alzheimer's. Mama could make you laugh so hard that you either had to hold your side or cross your legs and pray that you made it to the bathroom in time. I know that each of Mama's children got a portion of her comedic side (some more than others).

I am thinking of all of these things about Mama as I stood over the bowl of potatoes. I so much wanted to call my Mama to ask her about the ingredients for a potato pie. Before Alzheimer's, we talked several times a week. I was thankful when the phone company came up with long distance calling plans.

My yearning to call Mama was replaced with an ongoing flow of tears. I'm a grown woman with children of my own but I still wanted my Mama. I wanted to talk to her and to tell her something funny about what I thought was the right ingredients for my pie. I would have asked her if I should use buttermilk or olive oil just so that we could get a big laugh at how ridiculous my ingredients were. I was thinking that she probably would have laughed and said that I should just put the pie in the freezer if I put all of that stuff in it.

I wanted to call my Mama as I had always done several times a week throughout my marriage. Alzheimer's had taken over. I don't really know when the disease started. Items began to come up missing or we would find things in very unusual locations. She would have a shirt on backwards or she would have on a double layer of clothing. We loved Mama so much that I'm sure that there were many other signs that we simply overlooked.

We should have known that something was wrong when Mama started accusing Daddy of doing things that were just unbelievable. I started to get angry with Daddy for doing the things that Mama accused him of. I couldn't believe that he had turned into such an uncaring husband to Mama. The stories about Daddy got more and more outrageous. Mama would call the police on Daddy. She accused him of things that I dare not write. I wondered how Daddy could do the things to Mama and then act like the same loving father that we knew.

Mama is so strong that I believe that she knew that something was wrong, but she hid it from us. She fought Alzheimer's without knowing what she was fighting.

I began to see the toll that Mama's illness was taking on Daddy, my youngest sister, Dianne, and the rest of my sisters and brother. The many nights that Mama walked away from home are scary to think about even now. Our family is so blessed to not have received a late night phone call informing us that Mama had been hit by a car or bitten by a dog or fallen in a ditch or any other horrible catastrophe. When she could still dial the phone numbers, Mama was a constant voice on the other end of the phone talking about strange and unbelievable things that Daddy and others had done.

In a selfish way, I sometimes think that I'm glad that I didn't know the signs earlier because I would have known sooner that my Mama was leaving us. I might have fallen apart just knowing that my mother would stare at me and not know that it was me as she fondly called me "my seventh child".

Mama had finally come up against something that she couldn't create a remedy for. Alzheimer's had Mama in an unfamiliar position. There was nothing that she could do to control it. She put up an extremely strong fight but there I stood over a bowl of sweet potatoes, an indirect victim of Alzheimer's.

Through Alzheimer's I still recognize and give honor to God for His goodness. Mama often reminded me to pray and stay close to God and to love my family. Even with Alzheimer's disease, Mama never forgot her God. Her sentences would cover different periods of her life but the one aspect of her life that she consistently remembered was God. I realized that God carried Mama throughout her illness.

Mama always told us that if you look hard enough you'll find that you can always find something good in something bad. I had to look deep in this thing called Alzheimer's. What could I find good out of this bad thing that had happened to my Mama? The one thing that I could find in all of this was the fact Alzheimer's didn't allow Mama to feel the hurt of Daddy's death. She did not cry out for him when we rolled her close to his casket to say goodbye. I guess you could call that the good out of something bad. If Mama could comment on the matter, I know that she would find a list of good in her situation. She would tell you that she is still here for her children to hug and cling to a little while longer.

I know that God understands Mama's mumbled words when we don't. I know that God eases Mama's pain and allows her to sleep peacefully. Mama has been blessed to live well over three score and ten that Psalms 90:10 tells about. Mama is blessed and in turn we are blessed.

I gave the potato pie assignment to my son and daughter. They used a recipe book.

My Foundation

A Lesson On Truth

Fridays

The Countdown

Blow the Horn

The Magic Flute

A Lesson On Truth

Ok, I lied. To a shaking, trembling six year old, it seemed like the best thing to do. I knew that once Sallie Mae McKinney knew the truth, I would be in for it anyway. It became very obvious to me that I didn't think this through, especially after I received the worst whipping that my mother would ever give me.

To me, wasting a full bottle of nail polish far outweighed telling Mama a little white lie. Sallie Mae was someone who believed that if a child would lie to their own mother, they would lie to anyone. One of Mama's quotes growing up was "wrong doing will walk you down". This was certainly true on this day. She would also say that the truth would set you free. Mama would not uphold a lie but if you were truthful, she would defend you all the way to the highest court if she had too.

When I saw that I could easily open the bottle of crimson red nail polish, my only concern was how pretty my nails would look once I had finished polishing all of them red. In my mind, I saw ten shiny perfectly polished tiny nails.

I took my time and gave each nail special care. Somehow my caution did not stop the polish from smearing onto my fingers. The first try at this newly acquired skill looked bad even to a six year old. I figured that a quick wipe off with my shirt would give me a chance to start over. My plan was to just put my shirt with the rest of the dirty laundry for washing.

The second try wasn't any better than the first. I didn't like the way that my nails looked and I was quickly losing interest in trying a third time. Besides, the smell from the turned over bottle was more than I could bear.

I twisted the top back on the near empty bottle of nail polish, all the while getting crimson red polish on me and my clothes from the spill. I had an eerie feeling as I put the bottle back to where I found it. I shrugged off the eerie feeling and ran outside to play in the much needed fresh air.

I could hear Mama before I saw her. She wasn't looking at anyone specifically as she scanned the faces. She wanted to know who went in and made a mess with the nail polish. My sisters didn't waste any time saying,"I didn't". Just seeing the expression on Mama's face become angrier after each response and hearing the tone of her voice made me grab hold of silence and not let go.

I didn't say a word hoping that Mama would think that one of the "I didn'ts" was mine. This worked for about a minute.

Mama's anger soon turned to rage as she sternly told all of us to get into the house. I held on to silence a little tighter. As I struggled to hold on to silence, fear took hold of me. So there I was with fear and silence wrestling with each to see which would be the one to break me.

We all lined up in the family room and stood at attention like soldiers. Mama seemed to have grown an entire foot the one time that I finally took my eyes off of the floor. My eyes robotically went from the floor past Mama's house shoes, past the heaving chest, past the stiff neck, past the tightened lips, all the way to the glaring eyes of an army colonel surveying the lineup.

I could hear each one of my siblings repeat their negative answers. This time Mama looked each one of us in the eyes and repeated her question. I was forced to let go of silence because Mama asked me directly while staring me in the eyes, "Patsy, did you go in the nail polish?"

In my mind, the value of the polish was greater than the value of the truth and besides how would she know since I had wiped all of the polish off of my nails. I wasn't as eager as the others with my "no" but I gave the same answer. My mother repeated the question to me. Again, I along with the fear that was still present, chose to stay consistent with the other "no's". Mama then told me to hold out my hands. I didn't hesitate to stick them out because I knew that I had wiped the polish off with my shirt. Mama's glare quickly made me realize that I didn't do a very good job of wiping away all of the evidence.

By now all eyes were on me. Telling a lie didn't feel good at all. Mama had a look on her face that wasn't one of anger anymore. Later, I would realize that Mama's look was the look of disappointment. I had done the unthinkable. I had lied to my Mama.

The tears started before the first smack was ever felt. I don't even know where the belt came from. All of the time that Mama hit me, she never mentioned wasting or making a mess of the polish. Mama did like every other black mama in my era and lectured me with every lick of the belt. She seemed to give a smack with each word. You-better-not-ever-lie-to-me-while-you-on-this-earth-no-good-ever-came-to-a-child-that-would-lie-to-they-mother-you-gon-re-mem-ber-this-day-and-think-long-and-hard-before-you-lie-to-me-again-if-you-lie-to-your-mama-you'll-lie-to-any-one!

On this day, I decided that I would never ever lie again. That whipping changed my life. I can't say that I never lied about anything after that but I sure didn't lie to Mama. I have found myself quoting "if you will tell a lie to your mother, you will lie to anyone" to my kids and to other people.

Mama talked to me while combing my hair about the whipping. She wanted to make sure that I understood why she had to be so hard on me. More importantly, she wanted me to understand the consequences of lying. I know that I didn't understand on her level but I certainly understood that I didn't ever want to feel like that again. I remember the disappointment on Mama's face more so than the anger. I learned a lesson in truth from Mama and it was a lesson that helped me to be a better person.

Fridays

I remember as a child too young for school that Friday was a day that I along with my sisters and brother looked forward to. Daddy worked at a welding factory about three miles from our house. I don't know the exact time of the evening that Daddy ended his shift but I remember that he normally got home while it was still daylight. On most days we played outside after school and after completing homework. We were not allowed to sit around the house and watch television.

Our house sat on a hill so we could see Daddy coming way before he got to our short twisted driveway. There was a very large oak tree near our house that provided a convenient unfurnished tree house. There was usually someone up in the tree house but always on Fridays. When Daddy was spotted from the tree house lookout gallery, we would all stop whatever we were doing and then we would run as fast as our legs would carry us to meet the family's blue and white Oldsmobile at the foot of the driveway. The Oldsmobile was slowed down to a crawl as Daddy gave each one of us a chance to climb on top of the hood or whatever we could hold on to. I don't know how he knew when everyone had gotten on securely enough to take the ride up the hill. The Oldsmobile inched its way up the hill like a giant ladybug. This was such a thrill to us. No ride at the State Fair could be compared to our ride up the hill on the Oldsmobile.

When we finally made it up to the top of the hilly driveway, we piled off the Oldsmobile just as quickly as we had piled on. Neither of us waited for the other to climb down safely before we made our way to Daddy. We knew that on Fridays, Daddy would exit the car with a treat.

We gathered around Daddy as he pulled out the small brown paper bag filled with goodies. Daddy would change the treats up each week, so we didn't know if we would get a Hershey's chocolate bar, Mr. Goodbar, M&M's or our favorite, coconut Bon Bons.

As I think back on those Fridays, I remember the first life lesson on patience that I would recall. On one particular evening of our Friday treats, Daddy had brought the coconut Bon-Bons. When he brought this particular treat, everyone jumped up and down calling out for the pink coconut Bon-Bon.

The Bon-Bons came in an assortment of colors and I am pretty sure that they all tasted the same, but there was something special about the pink ones. As I think back on the rationale for the honor that we gave the pink Bon-Bons, I realize that we made the pink ones special just because.

I remember thinking to myself that I really really wanted that pink Bon-Bon. I must have been around five or six years old as I watched my siblings jumping up and down in front of Daddy. I decided that I would just wait and be content with the white one or the yellow one. I was outnumbered and was too far in the background of the bobbling heads vying for the pink Bon-Bon. I certainly would not be heard over the others.

I don't know if Daddy caught a glimpse of the disappointment on my face or if he had been paying attention to who was doing what all along. Much to my delighted surprise, Daddy reached over the heads of my siblings and handed me the beautiful pink Bon-Bon. Daddy told me that since I had waited patiently and had not jumped all over him, I got to have the pink one.

Daddy didn't stop and make a lengthy fatherly speech or anything. Besides, the others could not have cared less about my great achievement. This also did not stop this same routine on the Fridays to come but for me, Daddy's words were ones that I would always remember as my first life lesson on patience.

The Countdown

Mama is at the heart of two major count downs in my life. A countdown for me was a technique that I used when I was faced with an event that I was afraid of. My count downs were planned and well thought out.

The first countdown happened when I was only four years old. Yes, I can clearly remember so far back because it was a countdown event. I don't remember a build up to this day. All I recall is that I somehow figured out that my older sister, Celestine, was getting married to the man that kept kissing me on the jaw whenever I saw him. His name was Walter but everyone called him W.L.

I remember feeling all dressed up in a white dress. I remember that the sun was shining brightly and there were a lot of people outside. I remember seeing 'Lestine walking up to stand beside W.L. I remember 'Lestine telling me to "stand there" sometimes earlier. I didn't know why I was supposed to "stand there". I didn't know why until I saw her standing beside W.L. smiling and gazing into his eyes as another man with a bible did a lot of talking.

I started to feel uneasy and at that moment, I decided that I didn't want to "stand there" anymore. I was four years old and I clearly remember panicking. I remember thinking that my 'Lestine was leaving me. Celestine was my older sister. She was sixteen years older than me. Some people say that the rumor was that I was actually Celestine's baby and Mama was claiming me to be hers. That wasn't true of course.

Anyway, so I'm "standing there" as a flower girl in Celestine's wedding and she is gazing up at W.L. I decided right then and there that I didn't like W.L. anymore. I was still in a panic and nobody seemed to care or even notice. I remember looking around and thinking that I had to do something other than just "stand there". Hence, the countdown.

I had to think fast. The man with the bible needed to stop talking. 'Lestine needed to stop looking at W.L. like they were the only two people in the world. I clearly remember thinking that I would do a countdown and when I finished, I would cry for all of the world to hear. I would cry so loud that 'Lestine would have to stop gazing at W.L. and pick me up like she always did.

I put both hands behind my back. I don't remember if I counted correctly or not but I remember using my fingers on one hand that was still behind my back. I knew that if I counted out loud people would figure out what I was doing so I chose to keep my mouth closed during the countdown and to just think out loud. So here I go. Folding a finger into my palm with each number, the countdown began. Four-three-two-one! When I got to the number one, the emotions had built up so that I opened my mouth up as wide as humanly possible. I let out a scream for the entire world to hear. So far my countdown was going as planned.

As I waited for Celestine to stop the wedding, I felt a large hand cover my mouth so tightly that the people acted like they could not hear me. I tried to scream louder but the hand had muzzled all the sound from my opened mouth. It was Mama's hand and in one swift motion, she plucked me out of the wedding and had me inside the house within seconds.

Now the average Black woman in that era would have broken a piece off of the oak tree on the way inside and would have proceeded to give me something to cry about. Mama could have and should have done just that but she didn't. I believe that Mama looked past the fact that Celestine had me spoiled and saw the hurt of a four year old. I had showed out at the wedding but I believe that Mama somehow understood my panic.

Mama sat me down in the kitchen at the handmade wooden dinner table. She opened my hand and sprinkled a little baking soda on my palm. She told me to lick it so that my stomach would feel better. I didn't know how Mama knew that my stomach felt like butterflies were flying around it. I remember the soothing effect that Mama's words had on me.

My countdown had backfired on me. The wedding went on without me as a flower girl but I did get to go back outside as Mama had promised. A little baking soda and water plus the soothing love of my Mama had fixed everything. W.L. gave Celestine a mushy kiss and they had a long and happy marriage.

The second countdown happened when I was nine years old at the Bright Chapel M.B. Church in Byhalia, Mississippi. It was the week of the annual revival that was always held in the fall of the year. Our church was about a thirty minute drive from our home. The ride to church seemed like it lasted over an hour when you were packed in a station wagon with eight others. Revival meant that we had to take that ride every night for an entire week.

Revival service at Bright Chapel M.B. Church meant that lost souls would be sitting on the Mourner's Bench trying to make a spiritual connection with God so that you could become a convert. A convert was the holding stage before you got baptized. It meant that you had connected with God and now you just had to be dipped in the water. This would be the year that I found myself as a lost soul on the Mourner's Bench. Nancy, my eleven year old sister was also on the Mourner's Bench ready to make the conversion from sinner to convert. When Reverend Cole called for the sinners, I don't know if Nancy got up first or if I did. All I know is that I ended up on the Mourner's Bench with Nancy and about ten other lost souls.

I remember thinking that the church setting seemed like something off of a Tarzan movie with a crowd of people gathered around the lost souls singing. Even now, I can hear "couldn't hear nobody pray, oh oh down in the valley by myself, I couldn't hear nobody pray" in my mind as I write. I also remember that when you found the courage to get on the Mourner's Bench, you pretty much had to shout to get off and sit in the convert section. If you were still on the Mourner's Bench on Friday, you had to be full of sin. Each night the singing got more and more intense. I knew that I didn't want to still be on the Mourner's Bench on Friday.

On the first night of revival, I could see two of the lost souls getting their shout on. After they finished getting their shout on, they were asked some questions about whether or not they accepted Jesus. After they gave their teary answers, I looked up in the choir stand that was transformed to the Convert Section and there sat the two lost souls. They had made it. They had been converted and were taken off of the Mourner's Bench. I knew that I had to get me a plan. Hence, the second countdown.

Now for clarification, I must insert here that revival and the Mourner's Bench was a tradition in our church. I clearly remember accepting Christ in my life when I was seven years old. I had heard Mama and Daddy pray throughout my life. My Mama talked about her God a lot and one day when I was seven, I asked Mama's God to help me and He did. My heart was opened to God then and I have been saved ever since.

On Tuesday night, the second night of revival, I decided that I would do a countdown. At the end of my countdown, I would shout my way to the Convert Section.

When the singing started, I knew that I didn't want to sit through another night as a lost soul on the Mourner's Bench. So the countdown began. This time I counted down from ten. I was already crying when I got to five and by the time I got down to one, I was jumping up and down as if I had an invisible jump rope. In the middle of my jumping I felt some arms come around me and I could hear a woman crying who sounded like Mama. When I opened my eyes, I saw that the woman crying was Mama. I remember feeling a sadness come over me because Mama was holding me and thanking God. Mama held me so close that I could feel her heart beat. My countdown had backfired again. Sure, it had worked but I hadn't planned on the emotions that I felt as I clung to Mama.

I had done my countdown and I made it to the Convert Section after answering the questions. I remember thanking God that

I had made it. I realized that I really did deserve to join the others in the Convert Section.

Bright Chapel M.B. Church no longer requires the lost souls to sit on the Mourner's Bench in order to become members of the church. All you have to do is accept Christ in your life and in your heart as your Savior. I did that when I was seven years old. The second countdown helped me to survive a church tradition and it helped me to know that I had been converted.

Mama's daily talks about her God planted the seed for me. That is the best gift that she could ever give me.

Blow The Horn

Some traditions are passed down from one generation to the next but I can take the credit for starting this one.

The first time that I packed up to head to Johnson State University, I remember the day to be a Sunday. I had auditioned for a band scholarship and was anxiously preparing to go and join the Sonic Boom of the South. I knew absolutely nothing about the Sonic Boom and very little about Johnson State University. I had only decided to go a few weeks prior to my departure. Originally, I was all set to attend Memphis Junior College. This would have been a twenty minute drive from home. Daddy was a diehard Memphis Junior College Tiger's fan. Mama had decided that if I went to Memphis Junior College I would be able to come home every weekend. On the contrary, I thought that it was time for me to go away to something different. Besides that, I was dating a very sweet young man but I was feeling like our relationship was not going to work out. I had decided to break it off with him. I also felt that distance and time would make the break up easier.

My band director at Orange Mound High School did all of the leg work for me to audition for a band scholarship at Memphis Junior College. I left the audition thinking that I did not want to play any version of "Dixie". I would have still gone to Memphis Junior College had I not been introduced to Mr. Henry Houston. Mr. Houston was a vessel of fate. Johnson State University came to Orange Mound High School to recruit. They had never come before so I am convinced that God had a different destination for me. When I saw the film clip of Johnson State University, I was mesmerized at the band and the majorettes. The majorettes were called J-cettes. Sure, I would study Biology but I knew right then that I wanted to be a part of that band.

Henderson, my only brother, was assigned the job of taking me off to college. Henderson invited his girlfriend, Cynthia along. Back then, our parents had too many responsibilities at home to leave for a one day road trip. Henderson drove a small Vega. That car would never have held either of my children's college packings but I don't recall having to put anything back or to squeeze anything into the car. Everything fit in the compact trunk leaving the back seat just for me.

I remember having feelings of excitement, anticipation, and sadness all rolled up into one big emotion. Mama had prepared us food for the road. The aroma of the fried chicken was all through the house that morning but my emotions smothered any hunger pangs. I had spent the weeks leading up to that Sunday making sure that I was in shape for band camp. Daddy would look out the window and say "there she goes again" as I jogged around the house forty times twice a day. On that Sunday I felt sluggish as if everything was in slow motion. I was getting ready to leave home. I didn't know how I would feel being away so long.

Our house sat on top of a hill. As Henderson inched down the hilly driveway I looked back through the compact window of the Vega and saw a sight that I remember vividly to this day. Mama and Daddy stood on the porch waving. Daddy had a big proud smile on his face while Mama's wave was solemn. Mama's wave stopped and she sat in one of the chairs that we kept on the porch and began to sob. She always wore an apron while cooking and on this day the apron served as a handy handkerchief. When I saw Mama crying I felt like it was okay for me to let the tears drop and not feel embarrassed about Henderson or Cynthia seeing them. The back seat of the Vegas proved to be very useful to me on that day. I lay down on the back seat and cried myself to sleep.

The trips to Johnson State University created the same scene for many trips to follow. The driver would change but my look back would be of Mama wiping tears away with her apron. That is, until one Sunday evening I inched down the hill as the driver of a used Mercury Capri that Daddy had taught me how to drive the day before. I was an experienced driver but I had never driven a standard shift vehicle so I was quite nervous.

When I started down the hill, there Mama and Daddy stood again. Mama had her apron on ready to start wiping. I don't know what came over me but I started blowing the horn of the Mercury Capri. When I got to the bottom of the hill, I looked back up the hill and there was Mama and Daddy bent over laughing. This scene caused me to become very tickle and as I turned right onto Sandidge Road, my hand found its way back to the horn. I blew the horn until I was out of Mama and Daddy's view. My last sight of Mama was her laughing harder than I had ever seen. That scene helped to ease my nerves of driving to Jackson all on my own.

When I got back on campus and thoughts of Mama would cross my mind, I didn't picture her sad anymore. I pictured her laughing at me as I blew the horn all the way up Sandidge Road until I was just a speck in her view. I imagined that by blowing the horn, her worries were eased. I imagined that when she heard the horn she thought that I was a big girl now ready to take on the world.

From that day forward, I had a tradition. I would blow the horn anytime I got ready to head down the hill for Jackson. I expanded on my tradition and started blowing the horn when I arrived home. When Daddy heard my horn he would open the door with a big grin and tell me that he knew it was me.

Blowing the horn always brought out big smiles to the faces of my parents. I didn't stop blowing the horn when I graduated from Johnson State University. I didn't stop blowing the horn after I married and moved to Jackson. I didn't stop blowing the horn after I had children of my own and came to visit. I didn't stop blowing the horn after my granddaughters were born and I would take them to visit Mama and Daddy.

I knew that when Mama and Daddy heard the horn they had smiles on their faces. I didn't stop blowing the horn because it reminded me of them happy and laughing. That's how I wanted to remember them until I saw them again.

The Magic Flute

I was in the seventh grade when I started playing the flute. I was walking down the hallway, headed to my first day of Gym at East Side High School when I recognized the band director headed in my direction. The band director, Mr. Strong, was a tall stern instructor who was used to giving instructions to students without any challenge to what he told them.

Now, I expected to pass by Mr. Strong without being noticed, not that he would have any reason to notice me. I had heard about Mr. Strong's paddle so for that reason I was a little nervous as our steps put us closer and closer in proximity. My steps sped up as I tried to focus on the door leading to the gym. Although I wasn't looking forward to taking that gym class, it would be a welcome refuge.

East Side High School was actually all three grade levels combined. Elementary was in one section with Middle and High School each having their own section. School had only been in session for a little over a week but Mr. Strong already had the high school band out on the practice field every evening preparing for the first home game. My sisters, Clara and Tellie had graduated. Both played clarinet in the band under the direction of Mr. Strong. My brother, Henderson and my sister Nancy were the two current McKinney's who were in Mr. Strong's band. Henderson was an eleventh grade baritone saxophone player. Nancy played the oboe and bells. She was in her first year in the high school band as a ninth grader. Henderson and Nancy had told me about the paddle that Mr. Strong used on band members who did not follow his instructions. The mere thought of the paddle made going to the gym seem like a very good idea.

I thought that I must have misunderstood Mr. Strong because it sounded like he said my last name. My steps came to a halt when I clearly heard Mr. Strong say "McKinney"! I had only made it past him by a few steps so I knew that I was in reaching distance if he suddenly pulled out the paddle. I did not hesitate to respond back to him with a "Sir" without ever looking directly at him. He didn't wait for me to answer before he instructed me to go to the band hall. I looked towards the door to the gym and as if he were psychic, he told me that he would take care of that, meaning my excuse from gym.

I could hear the instruments playing before I got to the door of the band hall. I didn't recognize what they were playing but I would soon learn that they were warming up or rather, getting in tune prior to the start of rehearsal. Henderson and Nancy looked at me as if they were trying to tell me that I had wandered into the wrong room. Mr. Strong disappeared into his office and by the time that I walked across the band room to his office, he emerged from his office with a small slender horn case. He handed the case to me and told me to take the flute home and learn how to play it.

I took the flute from him and sat in a chair by the door. I was excited about learning how to play the flute as I waited for band rehearsal to end. Mr. Strong handed me a flute lesson book before I left to get on the bus to go home.

Along with my other siblings who played in the East Side High School band, my older sister, Celestine played the piano for as long as I could remember. She never once had a piano lesson but she could play as well or better than any other church pianist. I believe that it was the musical abilities of my older siblings that convinced or led Mr. Strong to give me such bold instructions.

As a small child, I had learned to position my lips over a drink bottle to produce the sound of a fog horn. This was one of the many acts of self entertainment when you are outside thinking of ways to past the time during the hot summers. The first time that I tried to produce a sound from the flute, I knew that I had a long way to go but once I recalled blowing into the drink bottle and applied it to the flute, I was all set.

I practiced on that flute everyday during every free moment that I had. I don't recall anyone ever telling me to shut up during my practice sessions. I guess it was because music had always been a part of the McKinney household.

So this is how I came to play the flute. I remember after a couple of weeks, rehearsal had just ended. I sat in my usual chair by the door. Mr. Strong referred to each of the McKinney sibling as just "McKinney". On this day, Mr. Strong looked directly at me and said "McKinney, let me hear something". I pulled out the lesson book and started to play some of the songs in it. Mr. Strong had big eyes naturally but when I started playing, the expression on his face caused his eyes to poke out even more. When he finally let me stop playing, Mr. Strong kept saying "I don't believe this". I wasn't sure of what he was talking about. Mr. Strong told me that I needed to be at band practice the next evening.

I don't know how it was worked out but Mr. Strong arranged for me to be excused from Gym and substitute it for Band. This time when I went to band practice, I joined the big kids including Henderson and Nancy. Now remember, I was in the seventh grade but I was granted a spot in the high school band.

I enjoyed practicing with the band. Mr. Strong made sure that although I was the youngest member, I didn't have any trouble from the older kids, including Nancy. One day we were in the band hall and Mr. Strong saw Nancy push me. Nancy got a visit from the paddle.

One of my fondest memories of being in the East Side High School band as a seventh grader was getting to perform at the school "Jamboree". I recall how fascinated I was. Even as I write this I am envisioning the crowed gymnasium and I can hear each one of the songs playing in my head.

The following year, the schools were integrated. This meant no more Mr. Strong and no more East Side High School band. Mr. Strong was a major influence on me. His encouragement made me feel that I could play as well as anyone else in the band and because he made me feel like this, that is how I practiced and played.

I didn't play the flute again until ninth grade. Mr. Richard Norris was the high school band director of the integrated school, Orange Mound High School. He was also a very talented musician who played trumpet professionally. Mr. Norris was also a major influence in my high school life. Mr. Norris believed in me. His encouragement not only helped me musically but on a more personal note. I could be pretty shy but having the encouragement of people like Mr. Norris helped me to grow on the inside. Mr. Norris went above and beyond to make sure that I was the recipient of numerous opportunities to develop my music skills. He did some bold things back then. He personally drove another band member, Gary Hewett, and

I for six hours to compete in a State Band competition. We did a live recording and I was simply fascinated.

My first real dose of racism occurred during one of the trips that Mr. Norris provided. It was a county competition held on the campus of Ole Miss in Oxford, Mississippi. When Mr. Norris dropped us on campus, I checked into my room which was the typical college dorm room with two students assigned to each room. As it turned out, I was the only Black girl there so this meant that I would be assigned a white roommate. This didn't bother me because by then I was used to being one of only a few other Blacks at the various competitions. Besides that, I had white friends at school and Mama had many white friends as well.

I heard the lock turn to the door and shortly after, I saw a tiny girl with blonde hair drag a duffle bag across the room to the bed nearest the window. She didn't notice me nor my made up bed as she collapsed on her bed with a sigh of relief. I understood the sigh because the duffle bag looked like it was big enough for her to fit in it with room to spare. I don't know if it was my "hello" or her realization that there was someone else in the room that startled her the most. She did not respond with a greeting, instead with a question. "Are you Lynn McKinney?" I didn't answer right away because I was puzzled as to why her body language and facial expression appeared to be afraid of what my answer would be. I could barely get my response out before she grabbed the handle of the duffle bag and dragged it back across the floor to the door.

This time, the bag didn't give her as much trouble exiting as it had done on her entrance. She said something about excusing her while she went to get something for her upset stomach.

The second ex-roommate came in escorted by her parents. The parents were assuring the daughter that she would love the Ole Miss campus. I hadn't moved from my spot since the first ex-roommate left. The parents nor the daughter bothered to ask me if I was "Lynn McKinney", they just told her that a mistake must have been made on her registration because Becky Stanley was supposed to be her roommate. They did not excuse themselves, they just left. I waited in the same spot on my bed for the third roommate but she never came. I thought about one of Mama's sayings that "you can always find something good out of something bad" because I ended up with a room all to myself.

My ex-roommate experience was salvaged when a black female Freshman by the name of Shirley. I was very easy to spot when Shirley noticed me sitting alone in the cafeteria. She befriended me and took me under her wings while I was at Ole Miss for those few days. She introduced me to her friends and for the rest of the competition weekend, I ended up having a good time. I never forgot Shirley for that. Our paths crossed years later when Shirley married my boyfriend's roommate.

Mr. Norris treated Gary and me like we were his assistants. During my senior year in high school, I recall marching out on the field in a majorette uniform, carrying a flag, and then playing flute in the stands. Mr. Norris would even allow Gary and I to take turns directing the songs. Mr. Norris did so much made my senior year to make it a very special year.

As my senior year in high school neared its end, I decided that I would continue playing flute in the college band. I had gotten accepted into Daddy's beloved Memphis Junior College. Mr. Norris was the one who took me to audition for a band scholarship. My audition included a piece that I had to site read. It sounded like a rendition of "Dixie". I remember the awkward feeling that I had while playing the piece. Mr. Norris was excited and proud for me to be a part of the Memphis Junior College band. I never forgot Mr. Norris' positive influence in my life.

During the last few months of my senior year, my plans were in place to attend Memphis Junior College. One day, the seniors were called to an assembly and the college recruiters from Johnson State University were there. The JSU representatives showed a film that gave the highlights of the college. Included in the film was a clip on the JSU band, the Sonic Boom. This is when I first met the band director from Johnson State University, Mr. Henry Houston. After seeing the Sonic Boom and remembering the awkward feeling that I had auditioning for Memphis Junior College, I decided that Johnson State University was the place that I wanted to be.

When the time grew closer for me to report to JSU, there was one big problem. I had a band scholarship but I didn't have a flute. I had always used the school's flute. I didn't know what I would do because I figured that a flute cost more than my folks could afford.

One day, Mama and I happened to end up in a music store. She did not tell me where we were going when we left the house, I was just glad to get a trip to Memphis. There were all kinds of instruments on display. I went to the flutes and saw the different brands. My eyes went to a flute that had open keys. I had seen one of the white girls with an open key flute during one of the band competitions. I ran my fingers across it, knowing that I would never own it because it was probably the most expensive one there.

Mama and I left the store without buying anything. I was not disappointed at all because I did not think that we would buy anything from that store. I was well aware of the many jobs that both my parents had to hold down in order to take care of a household that included nine children.

A few weeks later, I was home with Mama when she asked me if I still wanted to play in the college band. I responded with a "yes". Mama then told me that if I was going to play in the college band, I would have to have what was in her hands. Mama handed me a horn case that looked like a flute case. I remember how happy I felt at that moment. My fingers trembled as I snapped open the closures on the case. When I opened the case, much to my amazement was the open key flute. Oh my God! Mama had bought me the flute that I would never have imagined getting. Mama was just as happy as I was. I don't know what my parents had to sacrifice in order for me to get that flute. My parents always made us believe that we were as good as anyone else. At that moment, I was not afraid to play in a college band because my Mama felt that I deserved to be there.

When I got to Johnson State University, I had to audition for a spot in the Sonic Boom. You had to earn the right to march in the Sonic Boom. If you didn't make the cut, you were an alternate. This meant that you could wear a uniform, march in, but not perform on the field. I was determined that I would not be an alternate. My open key flute intimidated some of the other flute players. They didn't know if I could play or not but they knew that I was serious if I owned an open key flute because it was a little harder to play than a regular flute. I made the cut for the band and I ended up being the flute section leader during my third year with the Sonic Boom.

I loved that open key flute and I still do. I loved my Mama even more for doing something so special and loving for me. I wish that I had told my mother many more time just how much my flute meant to me.

My magic flute remains one of my most prized possessions.

RAYMOND AND SALLIE

A Love Story

Independence Daze

A Christian Home

A Love Story

When Alzheimer's had really set in with Mama, I would watch Daddy as he patiently and lovingly attended to Mama. Sometimes Mama would be fussing at "Raymond" the whole time. But he would answer back in an apologetic voice that he didn't want to upset her. I knew in my heart that this was love.

I won't say that there weren't any rocky and stormy days as we discovered the many symptoms of Alzheimer's. There were times that Mama would call the police on Daddy. Although I did not witness it, I do believe that Mama had gotten violent with Daddy. My sisters told me that the neighbor called and said that Mama and Daddy were in the front yard causing a scene. I don't know what was really happening in the front yard, but I do know that Alzheimer's would sometimes make Mama forget how kind and loving she could be.

Alzheimer's had taken its toll on Daddy because it made Mama say and do things that were not becoming of her. I believe that it was their love story that kept Daddy dedicated and committed to Mama. Sometimes after my husband and I have an argument, I think back to Daddy and I pray that if I ever get sick that my husband will remember our love story and that he would be as loving towards me as Daddy was to Mama.

Alzheimer's was rough on the McKinney family but it sure didn't take away Daddy's love for Mama. I wish that I had written down everything that Mama ever told me about how she met Daddy and some of the events of her younger years. My two older sisters, Lena and Celestine, knew a lot about the early years because they remembered growing up with Mama and Daddy. Lena and Celestine are both deceased. I can only cling to what they told me and what Mama told me.

It sounds like something from a movie but I do remember Mama saying that she was walking along the road and Daddy rode up beside her on a bicycle. I believe that Mama was fourteen years old at the time. That would make Daddy fourteen also, depending how Mama was feeling at the time she told this story. Mama would sometimes challenge Daddy as to who is really the oldest between them. They were both born in 1925 according to their birth records. Mama was born in May and Daddy was born in September. This, according to Mathematics would make Mama about four months older than Daddy. I think that Daddy would playfully tease Mama about being older than him. It sure didn't help Mama's case very much when her hair started to gray and Daddy only had a few gray strands here and there. Even when Daddy passed at eighty-one, he had very few strands of gray hair.

Mama said that Daddy rode up beside her on his bike and asked her to be his girl. I don't know how much time elapsed between when they actually first met each other and when they actually married. I do know that Mama had two small children when they finally married. Daddy loved Lena and Celestine just like they were his very own. I don't know how old I was when I found out that Lena and Celestine had a different father. I can say that when I found out that it didn't matter and it never did. That was love.

I wish that I could write about a juicy love story that developed between Mama and Daddy. The truth is, I don't know the "juicy". I can imagine that Daddy knew all along that Mama was a bit domineering, okay, she was a bit bossy. I'm sure that she could talk his ears off but I am also sure that early into their relationship, Daddy realized that Sallie Mae Rogers had many qualities about her that he could not help but fall in love with. I am sure that Daddy saw that when Mama loved you, she loved you with every bit of herself. I would also bet that Daddy got a good taste of Mama's sense of humor.

Mama and Daddy were very young when they married. I remember Celestine telling me that Daddy's grandmother, Mrs. Charlotte Carter, loved my Mama as if she were her own daughter.

Daddy's mother, Ivory Carter, was only thirty two years old when she died of tuberculosis. I would not want to imagine how it would feel or what it is to lose your mother at such a young age. I believe that Daddy and his mother were very close. Daddy had one sister, Blanche. Blanche died at a very young age also, shortly after his mother. I believe that Mama, lovingly filled the void that Daddy must have felt after losing the two people in his life that meant more to him than anything. I imagine that Daddy found a love in Mama that was so strong that it eased his loss and helped him to handle the hurt. Mama could give you that kind of love. Thank God, Daddy was able to find the love that he needed, a true love in Mama.

Independence Daze

I remember each and every 4th of July as a family reunion. Independence Day was anticipated by everyone each year. Sure, we decorated the back yard in red, white, and blue but the signing of the Declaration of Independence barely crossed the minds of the McKinney's on this day.

Our house sat atop a hill so anyone driving down Sandidge Road could see the many cars and the many people gathered in the backyard of the McKinney's. A passerby would probably draw the conclusion that we were having a neighborhood celebration when the truth of the matter was that the majority of the people gathered on top of that hill was related to Raymond and Sallie McKinney in one way or the other. If we invited a friend on this day, our friends always left wanting to come back. There was so much packed in the day. There was the swing in the back and games for the kids, but the main attraction for the day was the talent show.

In the center of the 4th of July gatherings you would find Mama and Daddy. Mama and Daddy would have been up since the crack of dawn clearing off the backyard, setting up tables, and doing whatever else was necessary to bring their family together. After going to college, I was usually home from Jackson and I would be there to help but oftentimes neither of them bothered to wake me. Mama and Daddy were always so glad for me to be home that they did their best to give me a morning of rest.

The 4th of July celebrations with the McKinney's are memories that I will always treasure. I cling to the memories of the 4th of July even more nowadays because the celebrations are so different without the presence of my mother and father. The day is still celebrated with family. It always seemed like a family reunion from the pre-college years, the college years, and then the years after I got married and started a family of my own.

There was one facet of the 4th of July celebrations that was the highlight of the day. Everyone anticipated the talent show. Mama and Daddy would sit back and enjoy the annual talent shows. I would have to say that the McKinney talent shows helped us to overcome shyness or to performing in front of an audience. This would be where the little ones would make their singing, dancing or creative debut. Thinking back on some of those talent shows I remember how funny my two nephews, Chad and Bernard, looked doing a basketball routine. You were not allowed to boo anyone. If we laughed it was always with good taste. Mama and Daddy wouldn't have it any other way. Mama and Daddy would always encourage the kids and I think this is what made the kids want to come back year after year with an act. The McKinney siblings were always entertaining at these talent shows. Nancy performed her annual rendition of the country hit "Delta Dawn". Clara was the main attraction who took her Gladys Knight renditions very serious. Dianne and Tellie would provide the backup for Nancy. Their backup included a hillbilly dance routine that always had the audience in tears laughing. Sometimes I would join the backup but I was usually too tickle to join them. The sisters always came up with some impromptu act to entertain the crowd but Mama and Daddy seemed to be entertained the most. We all could carry a tune pretty well but we all were natural born comedians as well so a little singing with a lot of comedy was usually the norm.

The 4th of July celebration of 2007 is still one that I remember vividly. I remember thinking that I wanted desperately to take my granddaughters with me to spend the night with Daddy on the night before the big celebration. I could feel myself acting desperate to get my kids and granddaughters up to spend the night with Daddy and I couldn't explain why.

Mama had been in the nursing home for nearly two years now. We tried bringing her home for family gatherings but it proved to be too much for her. So this year, Daddy sat alone in the backyard. My prior trips home since Mama was admitted to the nursing home found Daddy with a daze of sadness about him. I knew that Alzheimer's was taking its toll on him. Alzheimer's had taken his soul mate.

Mama remembered him still but not as her loving husband. She remembered him but treated him like an abusive parent. Daddy didn't seem to let that bother him. He missed Mama and I could look through his daze and see the hurt. When I visited him, I would get up early like Mama used to do and cook him a country breakfast. This is something that I really enjoyed. Daddy would brag on my cooking and tell me that it tasted like Mama's. This seemed to get him out of his daze. I always stayed with him when I came home for the 4th of July and the other holidays. Our breakfasts became very special to me.

Daddy loved children and all the children that grew up with the McKinney's loved him back. Daddy bounced every baby on his knee and knew how to make every baby laugh and reach for him. I don't believe that there is a child that grew up in our family who Daddy didn't fix up a bike for. Daddy was "Big Daddy" to all of his children's offspring.

As I thought about Daddy and how sad he seemed to be, I was determined for my granddaughters to spend the night with him. There was always something about kids in the house that made Daddy happy. His look of sadness was on my mind and besides that I knew that my granddaughters would enjoy their "Big Daddy".

Daddy was up early in 2007 for the 4th of July celebration but on this day he sat in his chair in the living room in a daze. I got up early with him to start breakfast. He snapped out of his daze for a little early morning conversation. He remembered that he had a key to the house for me because I didn't remember if I still had mine. I wondered why he wanted me to have that key seemingly out of the blue.

One by one, my sisters and brother came up the hill to the house. Everyone came with a dish, decorations or a game. My nephew John sat up the microphones for the annual talent show. My sister, Tellie and my brother-in-law, Ricardo dueled for control of the microphone. Word got around that the talent show was getting ready to start. Everyone gathered around as the show started.

Dianne and Tellie were entertaining as usual. Prissy stood in for her mom, Nancy and sang a hilarious country rendition of "Delta Dawn". There were many good acts that followed but the one to remember for me was my two granddaughters, Jaden and Jamie along with their cousin and my great nephew, Rock. Jaden was the oldest at almost four years old and Rock and Jamie were both two years old so this singing trio was quite impressive. There were three microphones and each stood in front of one and sang "This Little Light of Mine" like they were an experienced trio. While they were singing Daddy sat looking in amazement. He broke out the biggest grin. He stood up and walked closer to the three children as if to make sure that he wasn't imagining them. I can't really describe or find the words for the peculiar emotion that I felt at that moment. Daddy seemed to be looking at those kids and seeing his family in the back yard for years to come. His dazed smile seemed to say "okay".

Daddy died less than three weeks later. Afterwards, as I sat in a daze, I thought back on that unusual 4th of July celebration and everything about that day made sense to me then. We didn't know that this would be the last 4th of July celebration with Daddy but God did.

A Christian Home

The thought of being raised in a Christian home when told to others could come off sounding dull, boring, or restrictive. That's because for some, to be raised in a Christian home means that you get religion shoved down your throat or rules so strict that many can't wait to leave home. In the McKinney household, a Christian home meant that love was at the heart of everything. God is love.

Raymond and Sallie McKinney were wonderful gifts from God to their children. Early on, neither Raymond nor Sallie was one to verbally tell you that they loved you but their actions let us know that we were loved. When Mama got older, she started to verbally say "Love you" a lot. I believe that as she started to have symptoms of Alzheimer's, she said it even more.

We were encouraged in love. The expectation from Sallie McKinney was that your family should cheer you on or be at events to support you when no one else was. This is something that I have instilled in my children. When a child is in a play or in a sport, they should be able to look out in the audience and see their family.

We were disciplined in love. No, they did not spare the rod, but thinking back on some of my whippings or my sibling's whippings, I can remember Mama and Daddy looking hurt or even being brought to tears after they finished. We knew that we had to be punished when we did wrong because that is what is expected in a Black religious family, especially in the McKinney family.

I remember one night Nancy had gone out and was way past her curfew of getting home. Mama paced the floor. I knew that it was major when Daddy got up from bed and waited in the living room near the front door. Mama went back to the bedroom as Daddy sat alone in the dark. I am sure that Mama didn't go to bed. I can say with utmost confidence that Mama went back to the bedroom to pray. Mama knew that the mild-mannered Raymond had left the building.

I heard the car coming up the hill. My heart was racing as I imagined Nancy getting out of the car and walking up the steps to the door. I could only imagine because I was too terrified to yell out the window to her although I desperately wanted too. I heard Nancy's footsteps as she headed towards the door. Mama did not come out of the bedroom.

The bedroom that I lay in had a window that was only a few feet from the front door so I could hear Nancy slowly turn the doorknob. I know that Nancy had to know that she was in trouble but she might have thought that she would buy some time since the house was dark. Maybe she thought that Mama and Daddy were in bed fast asleep and that she would experience their wrath the next morning. Nancy eased the door open just enough to ease her body in and make every effort to close the door back to its locked position.

Daddy didn't turn on any lights. Nancy didn't get a chance to close the door. Before she knew it, Nancy was ambushed by Daddy. I could hear the belt whisk through the air as each blow came down on Nancy. All I could hear was Daddy and the belt. Daddy was asking Nancy questions and Daddy was giving Nancy answers to the questions. Daddy's talking and the blows from the belt had a certain rhythm to it. It seems as though Daddy was keeping the beat in 4/4 time. Every four counts there would be a question or an answer. The thing that only made matters worse was the fact that Nancy didn't cry or run or scream. Nancy just ducked and covered. I cried for her. Mama cried for her. I don't know who else was awake and could hear what I was hearing because I wouldn't dare get up or try to interfere. Soon Daddy cried for her. I would not describe Daddy's demeanor as rage although I know that it was close. Daddy had rules for his house. He wanted us to do what was right and to respect him and to respect Mama. Disobedience was a sin and he just wasn't going to tolerate a disobedient child. He told Nancy that he would put her out. Nancy had disrespected Daddy's home by being out with a boy, staying out late with a boy, and now her silence to his chastisement was a new level of disrespect towards him.

Daddy did the ultimate and put Nancy out of the house. He stormed back to the bedroom with his footsteps down the hallway sounding like those of a giant. I could hear Mama trying to comfort Daddy and telling him that he was going to make himself sick. Mama now came out of the bedroom.

Mama was really the one who issued most of the whippings. Her whippings covered minor offenses like not washing the dishes or not sweeping the floor. Now the minor was bumped up to a major if you hid the dishes in the oven and she turned the oven on the next morning to the smell of burning plastic or cracking ceramic. Daddy was called in for the major whippings.

Mama knew that Nancy's offense on that night was an extreme major one. Mama had tried on many occasions to talk to Nancy about being so headstrong. Nancy had toughness about her not like any of the other children. I don't even know why she was out on a date at fifteen but I know that she could handle herself wherever she was. Mama had to allow Daddy to give Nancy some tough love that night because Nancy needed to know that the choices that she made had consequences.

Mama walked with a quickness to the front door. As a mother, I can imagine that she was frantic that Nancy might have run away. The Lord was the only One who Mama could ask for help as she opened the door to look for Nancy. The Lord didn't make Mama wait for an answer because when she opened the door, there sat Nancy on the steps. Nancy's toughness had disappeared as tears rolled down her face. Mama called Nancy's name as if she was making sure who Nancy was. She told Nancy to get in the house. Mama didn't hug Nancy then but I know that she wanted too. Discipline was serious and obedience had to be taught. This is something that was passed down from their parents and the people that helped to raise them.

All of the madness on that night was love in action. Our parents knew that without discipline and obedience there would be a tough road to travel. I knew that on that night, as bad as it seemed, it could have been worst. Daddy could have met Nancy's boyfriend, Charles with a loaded shotgun.

Daddy was known for his shotgun and rightly so with eight girls under one roof. I remember my sister Clara hosting an outside party. Most of the guests drove cars up the hill but before the night would end the guests ran down the hill leaving the cars behind. Daddy had told them that the party was over and the guests were not leaving fast enough. Daddy's first shot got everybody's attention. The second and third shots sent everyone running down the hill. That was the last party at our house.

Yes, Charles was lucky that night. The lesson that Daddy wanted to give was for Nancy not for Charles. Daddy said that a hard head would get you in trouble and out of love he didn't want that for Nancy.

The rules were strict and even stricter for me. I believe that Mama and Daddy blamed themselves for Nancy getting pregnant and marrying at such a young age and I would soon learn that I had to suffer the consequences. It took me years to realize that that was love.

Neither mama nor Daddy got more than an eighth grade education but both had a burning desire for their children to be well educated. Mama offered wise Christian advice whenever we went through a life event and went to her for comfort. Daddy kept us grounded by having us to read the bible together as a family. When we were younger he would have us read the bible to him. As we got older, it was always a welcomed treat to read to him. My brother, Henderson, often read with Daddy so that he would be ready for Sunday school.

Our Christian home is one that was never dull and never boring. Raymond and Sallie Mae McKinney planted the seeds in their children to seek Christ and the love of God. Our parents showed love and most importantly, they sowed love. This love is what led us to Christ. God's love has sustained us through Alzheimer's.

SOMETHING GOOD OUT OF SOMETHING BAD

Courage

Courage

It has taken a tremendous amount of courage for me to write this chapter for this book. Usually I am not this indecisive but for this I had to dig deep and find some "Sallie Mae McKinney" kind courage. Writing this chapter will allow you as the reader to know something that I have not openly discussed with anyone since it happened in the summer of 1966 in Orange Mound, Mississippi. I did not want to write this chapter because I didn't want to have to remember what happened. I even delayed trying to get this book published because of this chapter. As I sat in church one Sunday, God made it clear to me that my focus of this chapter should not be so much as to what happened but more so of what did not happen. God protected me from something that could have been horrible and even tragic.

I was only nine years old and I had spent the night with my oldest sister, Lena. Lena was married to Thomas and they lived on East Sandidge Road. My parents and the rest of our fourteen member household lived on West Sandidge Road. By this time Lena had four children. Jeanette was the oldest at seven and the other three followed in age in two year increments.

Both East and West Sandidge Road were integrated with both black and whites living on the road. On our end, West Sandidge, the whites lived right in the middle of the blacks on both ends of the road. The Wallace family was a white family that lived on West Sandidge. Mama and the matriarch of the Wallace family became very close friends. Mrs. Wallace lived to be in her early nineties. I would even go so far as to say that before Mrs. Wallace died, she and Mama had become best friends. Mama sat with the Wallace family at Mrs. Wallace's funeral.

On this particular visit with Lena, all of the children including me were outside playing in the front yard. Lena, like other mothers, did not allow children to run and play in the house. Lena's house was a small house with only a living room, two bedrooms, and a kitchen. When you walked into the house through the screen door, you would be looking directly into her main bedroom because there were no doors. Unlike our house that sat up on a hill, Lena's house sat only a few yards from the road. As we ran and played outside, a car caught my attention because it had traveled back and forth past Lena's house. The car was a white station wagon with writing on the side. At about the same time that I noticed the car, Lena stepped outside and told us to go inside because she was going to pick Thomas up from work. Lena didn't normally keep the family's only car but on this day she had done some cleaning for Miss Celia, the white lady who lived up the road from her house. Miss Celia was very fond of Lena and she often gave Lena hand-me-down clothes for the kids. Lena's instructions got a little sterner as she got into the brown Oldsmobile and turned on the ignition. Lena told us to go inside one last time before backing onto the road this time instructing me to get everyone inside. As Lena's car made its way towards L&M factory, I saw the white station wagon past Lena's house again. I saw that the car was driven by a white man and the man looked me directly in the eyes. It was a scary look that made me yell to the others to come on and get inside. As we all ran to the screen door, the white car pulled into the yard and the plump white man got out of the car and came right up to the door. We had all made it inside the house when the man got to the screen door. The man asked me if my mother was home. This a time that I know that God interceded and gave me the words to say. I developed a relationship with God when I was seven years old. Mama and Daddy had planted the seed. I knew God and I knew that He was real. When that man asked me if my mother was home, I pointed to the L&M factory and told him that Lena was right over there and that she would be right back. I remember telling him to look right over there. Trembling, my eyes focused on the latch to the screen door as the man asked me if I wanted some bubble gum. By the time I answered "no", the man had burst through the screen door before I could get my trembling fingers to the latch. I remember hearing Lena's children scream and run towards the kitchen. I screamed as the man grabbed me and literally tossed me in the air onto bed in Lena and Thomas' bedroom. I remember that the plump white man wore glasses and had on brown pants with a black belt and a white shirt. The plump white man with the black glasses, white shirt, brown pants and black belt, laid on the bed beside me. I could only scream but during my screaming, I thought about God. I screamed to God and God heard me. The plump white man with the black glasses, white shirt, brown pants and black belt jumped up as if he heard someone coming. I know that he had to be thinking that he only had a few minutes since I repeatedly told him that Lena would be right back and you could actually see the L&M factory from Lena's house. The plump white man with the black glasses, white shirt, brown pants and black belt had planned on committing a horrible crime that day but God said "No!" God had saved me. I knew it then and I know it even more today.

I remember getting up running in a daze when the plump white man with the black glasses, white shirt, brown pants, and black belt, jumped in the white station with writing on the side. I looked for Lena's children and found them huddled together outside, all crying. I gathered them together and told them to come on. We walked through a path to Miss Celia's house. Through our screams and tears, Miss Celia was somehow able to understand that a white man had broken in and thrown me on the bed. I am sure that Miss Celia was certain that I had been raped. Miss Celia was very comforting to us, telling me that everything would be all right and that she would get Sallie Mae for me.

I don't remember how long it took for Mama to come for me. I don't remember Lena coming to Miss Celia's house. I just remember Mama hugging me and crying. I don't remember going to bed that night or anything after reaching Miss Celia's house. I just remember Mama taking me to the doctor's office. There was a black nurse there who came in the room with Mama. First the nurse asked me if he took my panties off. I don't remember saying anything to the nurse. Mama held me and asked me if the man took his pants off. I remember telling Mama "no" because I remembered the brown pants with the black belt. I don't remember everything that Mama asked but I remember her asking me again if he took his pants off. I don't remember getting checked but I'm sure I must have been. I remember the nurse telling Mama that I was all right and that she could take me home.

Mama's strong faith in God is what gave her the strength to maintain her composure, her will, her sanity. Mama didn't want her little girl to feel like she was a pitiful little girl afraid to live like a normal little girl. Mama wanted her little girl to grow up jumping, skipping, and playing just like any other normal little girls. Mama's courage is what was needed to simmer the rage of a father whose little girl had been violated. Mama was the only one who could assure Daddy that their little girl would be alright. Mama did not want to see her husband or her little girl's father go to jail or be killed for taking out his rage on the plump white man with the black glasses, white shirt, brown pants and black belt. Mama knew that Daddy and his cousin Lawrence would continue to ride the East and West Sandidge Roads until they found the plump white man with the black glasses, white shirt, brown pants and black belt until they brought justice to him. Mama had to have the courage to see past Daddy's rage so that her little girl and her eight other children would grow up with the love of their father.

Mama's strength and courage sustained me. It shielded me from the sick world of the plump white man. Mama's courage helped me to put away that day at Lena's house. That day was never forgotten but the memory of it was overshadowed by the loving upbringing of my parents. God's protection is what saved me. If Mama had not had the courage to pray me through that awful incident, I am sure that my life would have been very different.

And so I have decided to quit stalling and to find the courage to go forward with completing this book. This chapter has held my progress up for several years. It's ironic that this chapter's title is the very thing that has been keeping me from completing my work. As I think about Mama, I have found the courage to move forward. Mama would say that I have to focus on the good and that is that because of God's grace I was not raped on that day. Yes it was scary and bad but it could have been a whole lot worse.

Mama didn't talk to me about the plump white man with the black glasses, white shirt, brown pants, and black belt for a very long time. Twenty five years passed before I would talk to her about it again.

SOMETHING EXTRA

Mama Said…..

Mama Said

I am constantly reminded of words that were spoken by Mama. I am sure that each one of Mama's children, grandchildren, and great grandchildren can write their own chapter about what Mama said. Sometimes Mama would say something to you that you really didn't want to hear, but you always knew that she was right.

There are two simple phrases that Mama would quote that I would have to say that have helped to shape my character. Nothing elaborate, just two simple phrases.

The first phrase is only four words- "Do what is right". The phrase may not be grammatically correct but it sounds perfect to me. I cannot number the times when this simple phrase knocked the little red devil off of my shoulder. I know that

I like anyone else, have many flaws, but hearing my Mama's words echoing in the back of my mind has helped me along this journey called life. Oftentimes when I watch the news and I hear about politicians getting caught in their wrong doings or corruption uncovered in large corporations, I say to myself, if only they had heeded Mama's advice.

The second phrase is only one powerful word. Pray. This advice applies to any and every situation in life that you may encounter. When you pray about a situation, you are acknowledging that you believe that God will hear you. Praying allows you to let God bear your burdens. Before making any major decision-pray. Before facing obstacles-pray. When you're happy-pray.

Mama said a lot of things. Some were serious. Some were comical. Some were downright confusing at times but if Mama said it, I believed it.

"Wrong doing will walk you down"

"Don't worry about how they treat you, you just worry about how you treat them"

"Goats to the left and sheep to the right"

"Babies have rights too"

"Be weary of a too jealous man cause he probably is doing something he aint supposed to be doing"

"Make your food look pretty and it just might taste pretty"

I asked my brother and sisters for some of their memorable Mama Said phrases.

Clara: "Mama used to say that sometimes you have wink at the world". Sometimes people will try to use you to satisfy something on their agenda but when you know that you're actually working your own agenda and the user is supplying the resources, just wink at the world.

Roz: "Mama said that you shouldn't sleep on your rights". This simply meant that you have to speak up for yourself because if you don't, the world will just pass you by and someone else will speak up in your stead.

Dianne: "Mama said to pay your bills on time". Don't create bills that you cannot pay. Most of the time, you can do without if you just give yourself a little time between seeing and buying. Mama believed in having good credit. She could walk into any bank and get approved because she built up a reputation of never being late for payment.

I actually could write a book entitled "Mama Said" because she is the wisest woman that I have ever met. The memories of my mother have inspired me to complete something that has been near and dear to my heart and that is to write a book. I am very thankful that my first book is centered around the one who holds my heart, my Mama. I remember everything about her. Her laugh, her cooking, her sense of humor, her talents, her bravery, and her spiritual gifts. I remember Mama's love.

As I remember, I hope that you, the reader will take the time to write down the things that you remember about your loved ones.

I pray that there will one day be a cure for Alzheimer's disease. Alzheimer's robs its victims of their memory but it cannot take away the lasting memories of each person who is stricken with the disease.

My Journal

_____

_____

_____

_____

_____

_____

_____

_____

_____

_____

_____

_____

_____

My Journal

My Journal

My Journal

_____

_____

_____

_____

_____

_____

_____

_____

_____

_____

_____

_____

_____

My Journal

My Journal

_____

_____

_____

_____

_____

_____

_____

_____

_____

_____

_____

_____

My Journal

My Journal

My Journal

My Journal

_____

_____

_____

_____

_____

_____

_____

_____

_____

_____

_____

_____

_____

My Journal

Printed in the United States
By Bookmasters